D1266670

HE BECAME LIKE US

HE BECAME LIKE US

The Words of Identification

CARLYLE MARNEY

ABINGDON PRESS / new york / nashville

ABIGAIL E. WEEKS MEMORIAL LIBRARY
UNION COLLEGE
BARBOURVILLE, KENTUCKY

232.958
M353

HE BECAME LIKE US

Copyright © 1964 by Abingdon Press

All rights in this book are reserved.
No part of the book may be reproduced in any
manner whatsoever without written permission of
the publishers except brief quotations embodied in
critical articles or reviews. For information address
Abingdon Press, Nashville 2, Tennessee.

Library of Congress Catalog Card Number: 64-10603

SET UP, PRINTED, AND BOUND BY THE
PARTHENON PRESS, AT NASHVILLE,
TENNESSEE, UNITED STATES OF AMERICA

His most remembered words, and his most used words, wrenched out of him during his longest hours, are words of his identification.

HE BECAME LIKE US

For my MOTHER

For my MOTHER

CONTENTS

I. Father, Forgive Them   13

II. To-day Shalt Thou Be with Me   25

III. Behold Thy Mother   35

IV. My God, Why Hast Thou Forsaken?   45

V. I Thirst   53

VI. Father, into Thy Hands   61

VII. It Is Finished   67

VIII. Behold, I Show You a Mystery   73

And as they led him away, they laid hold upon one Simon, a Cyrenian, coming out of the country, and on him they laid the cross, that he might bear it after Jesus.

And there followed him a great company of people, and of women, which also bewailed and lamented him. But Jesus turning unto them said, Daughters of Jerusalem, weep not for me, but weep for yourselves, and for your children. For, behold, the days are coming, in the which they shall say, Blessed are the barren, and the wombs that never bare, and the paps which never gave suck. Then shall they begin to say to the mountains, Fall on us; and to the hills, Cover us. For if they do these things in a green tree, what shall be done in the dry? And there were also two other, malefactors, led with him to be put to death. And when they were come to the place, which is called Calvary, there they crucified him, and the malefactors, one on the right hand, and the other on the left.

Then said Jesus, Father, forgive them; for they know not what they do. And they parted his raiment, and cast lots.

—Luke 23:26-34

I

FATHER, FORGIVE THEM

So very much has gone on before we come on stage. The drama is all but over. It is midway in Act III. Again and again, during these days till Easter, we shall be asking ourselves, "What on earth is happening here?" And try to answer as we will, we shall only be successful in getting it said for today, for this week, for we shall have to ask it again and again in our lives.

What on earth is happening here? "The cross of Christ," says Paul Scherer, "was either a tragic incident which meant that his kind of life was tragic and impotent; or it was the supreme symbol of God's conquering presence in the world that he made, a mercy and justice and peace so closely akin to the Eternal that they could be nailed down and still win!"

So much has gone on before we come on stage. That week of tragedy began so bravely. Look how grandly it began. But do not all weeks of tragedy begin so? Do not all days of tragedy open with life breaking out onto some plaza, with crowds and palms and cries of Welcome! Welcome! Then comes some bitter, bitter halting of the parade. Floats grind to a stop. The rains wash away the banners and the decorations, and we have to sit it out in some antiseptic waiting room. Like Christ waiting before Pilate or some other judge, we too have to wait it out.

The trouble with life is not that there are too many lawyers. The trouble is that there are too many judges. We all have to wait before Pilate or some other judge: the surgeon or the specialist or the brain-man we sent for or the internist or the judgment in bankruptcy or the dread mental incompetence or the funeral home—so many judges around. Not too many lawyers, but too many judges. Pilate or Herod or the priests or the Romans or the high churchmen of one brand or another or the crowd—the fickle crowds. So many judges to wait before.

Yet Calvary was not "the normal outcome of a perfectly normal situation"—waiting before a judge. This hill where a man "far too good to be safe" was put to death was an unusual hill. This man "did something by dying." Not many men are too good to be safe.

There were three deaths on this hilltop, two kinds

of death. "On one, death came down with a taunt, like the world's last grin, dark and sterile and hopeless. On another it came in a sudden shaft of light, as of the sun striking its way . . . to etch out of the shadows," a pair of eyes that shielded a "brooding" glory. It took a bright light to see glory in those eyes. Between those two deaths, as far apart as time and eternity, as far apart as some of us from each other, the Word became deed indeed. This is what is happening there. But we came in so late, didn't we?

So much had gone on before: wine at a wedding feast and talk about a coming bridegroom, faith like a mustard seed, glory on a mountain, the bread of life, the water of life, the raising of Lazarus, the whipping in the Temple, the confrontation of the professionals, the founding of a fellowship, the sermon on the mountain, and the blessed last supper. So much had gone on before.

And so very, very much had already been said before we came on scene.

"The prince of this world cometh, and hath nothing in me." "I lay out for you a kingdom." "If ye love me, keep my commandments." "A new commandment I give unto you." "Henceforth I call you not servants, but [call] you friends." I am the vine, I am the door, I am the way, I am the truth, I am the light, you are a branch, you are a neighbor, you are a brother, you are a friend, you are salt, you are light, you are witness. Do you know what I have done to you? he says.

So many ways to ask what on earth is happening here. Through so many windows and doors we could look to ask, What is going on here? We might take these seven days to talk about the people he touched. Or we might talk about the people around the cross who refused to allow him to teach them and therefore opposed him. We might talk about the people who stood by grieving. Or we could use the days for meditation on the meaning of his life. We could talk about the things that he did: the healing signs that spoke of a Kingdom. Some year, perhaps, we may do the stations of the cross. Our way for this Easter journey, however, is different.

We are going to talk of the words people said he said. As they looked back over their shoulders, going away from Calvary, they knew they could never leave it for good. They would have to keep coming back by this place to look to see if it was still there. As they looked back at the cross they knew they could not ever leave for good; they remembered that he had said some words. We will use them to ask what on earth is happening here?

After they had lifted him up, after the wood had settled into the grip of the earth, after his body weight had sagged into the slots of agony that would encase him until blessed oblivion should come, he said—

they said he said—*"Father, forgive them; for they know not what they do."* This is a shocker, so much a shocker these words that the early church could not endure the memory of these words, and dropped them. They do not appear in Codex Vaticanus, or the earliest of Codex Bezae. A score of other important manuscripts do not show these words. *The words were hot and the church dropped them for a season!* For a man hanging in this slot of agony to cry, "Father, forgive them," this is too slippery, it is too sentimental, it is too sticky, but mostly it was just too much.

Early Christians just could not stand his forgiving Jews this way. They never aimed for it to get out. Not in the second century nor again in the ninth nor again in the twentieth did we aim for the word ever to get out, that he could forgive this way! The Christian church in its early years did not want him forgiving Jews this way—not to speak of Romans or Saxons or Jutes or Angles, like us, or Publicans or sinners or harlots or tax experts. The subsequent history of the Jews indicates that God had neither heard nor forgiven, for in less than forty years a bloodbath such as no city of his time knew had soaked Jerusalem from its edge to its center. The subsequent history of the church, too, indicates that it did no good for God to forgive the Jews. The world intended to wipe them out. Yet the persecuted church let the words stand in the best manuscripts, in the best tradition, in the best families of documents for they say something mighty about what on earth is happening here?

The main stream of Christendom, long since joined by the Roman tradition, has kept them, too, since these are not sentimental words or slippery words or sticky words. Nor is it too much that he would cry, "Father, forgive them." It is not the word of forgiveness that we cannot endure; *it is the great cry of identification that we have not yet been able to accept!*

When Jesus Christ cries, "Father, forgive them," somebody is joining somebody. Someone is getting on the side of someone. This is what it means. Someone is taking a stand with another who would otherwise stand in a very bad light. This is the one note we follow to understand what is happening here. It will appear in each succeeding cry. When he says, "To-day shalt thou be with me in paradise"; when he says to John the beloved, "Behold thy mother," and to his mother, "Behold thy son"; when he says, like a little baby, "I thirst"; when he says, "Father, into thy hands I commend my spirit"; when he says, "My God, my God, why hast thou forsaken me"; when he says, "It is finished"; every one of those in essence is the cry that betokens an unthinkable, unbelievable identification of the divine with the human. He joins somebody!

When he says, "Father, forgive them," he is telling the Father, on whose side he stands, the side of men like you and me. Somebody is joining somebody. 'Tis the one note we follow. Someone is identifying himself and his plight, his situation and his needs, his suffering with something that is already going on. He is joining the mass crucifixion that is going on in this world. Indeed it has been going on a long time.

Do you hear as I do? Here is a final token of his compassion shown in that hospital corridor which is an early chapter of Matthew. When he saw them with every illness and disease, the scripture says, "He was moved with compassion!" Do you hear it as I do? *It is a final coming to that Jerusalem that would not come to him.* On the low parapet over Olivet he had wept, "O Jerusalem, Jerusalem, which killest the prophets, and stonest them that are sent unto thee; how often would I have gathered thy children together, as a hen doth gather her brood under her wings, and ye would not!" So! The mountain will not come to Mohammed; then, Mohammed has come to the mountain! This is what it means. Here in this cry, "Father, forgive them," he joins Jerusalem. Jerusalem will not come to him; very well, he has come to her.

Father lay not this deed to their charge. Father I am on their side! Father this is what it is to be

man! It is to be hanged, it is to be caught, it is to be
stripped, it is to be nailed. Here he joins us forever.

Blessed Irenaeus was the first of the Fathers truly
to see this. Twice in his gigantic *Adversus Haereses*
he says, "What he appeared to be, that he was." Again
twice, he says, *"He was what he seemed to be."*
Earlier the letter to Hebrew Christians had claimed
that the head of our salvation was made complete in
his sufferings. He became like us, and "it was fitting."
Here then, more than at any other gate, at the very
lintel post to death, he joins us. He joins us, not by an
insipid "Let bygones be bygones," not by making
excuses and allowances for people to whom we are
related; nor did he mean the overlooking of my in-
laws' faults. Neither did he mean forgetting and smil-
ing, nor understanding and saying, "They are worth
it." This forgiveness is not sentiment; it is identification. He joins us in our situation, in our flood of
ignorance and trouble. For most of these crucifiers
would be crucified too. They stood there in their
blood—"when thou wast in thy blood," the classic
Hebrew had cried, "Live!" And now that the Hebrew
is present at the Crucifixion as Crucified saves neither
them nor us from crucifixion.

Will you take a short look at that ignorance which
I prefer to translate as that not-knowing of theirs?
Whether their unknowing or their misknowing or
their not-knowing be a "circumstantial" ignorance,
as with the soldiers, or a "judicial" ignorance, as

with the Jews responsible, or a "willful" ignorance, as with us, the pathos of the situation here is that we are all what Nicholas of Cusa called *doctors of ignorance*. Do we not all have Ph.D.'s in misknowing, not-knowing, and unknowing? Are we not all victims of that tragic ignorance which acts as if it were knowledge? Our misknowing and our not-knowing have nothing to do with it here. When he cries, "Father, forgive them, for they know not what they do"; here we have the elemental relationship expressed that whatever our condition, whatever your condition, he joins us! I do not have to go to him first; he comes to me.

So impressed was Irenaeus by this that he moved the Crucifixion farther toward us. He moved it forward more than twenty years and had Christ dying at fifty-five instead of thirty. So he said, Christ was a babe for babes, and a young man for young men, and a man for men, is it not reasonable that he would be an old man for old men? But no matter, "What on earth is going on here?"

One thing only. Here he joins us. No matter what our condition, here we are identified. Here we are *"them."* Father forgive *them,* Father forgive you, Father forgive these whom I have now joined; they do not know. Father forgive these for whom I am a mediation. Here he identifies himself with us. And here we identify with him. Here we can see him for what he is. Here we identify ourselves and return the favor by joining him. This some of you have done. But some have not and will not.

There is something left for you. Those of you who will not identify with him have something left. You may have what the watcher always divides after the play is over! And those who looked on, but did not identify, divided his clothes among them, by lot.

There are men and women in Christian churches who have been attending for years who go out, taking all they brought; but all they have is a piece of a leftover coat from somewhere. In his identifying with us it is expected that we shall identify with him. But the watchers divided the leftovers, and "they parted his raiment, and cast lots." For was this not all that was left? The rest of it had been identified with us sinners.

And one of the malefactors which were hanged railed on him, saying, If thou be Christ, save thyself and us. But the other answering rebuked him, saying, Dost not thou fear God, seeing thou art in the same condemnation? And we indeed justly; for we receive the due reward of our deeds: but this man hath done nothing amiss. And he said unto Jesus, Lord, remember me when thou comest into thy kingdom. And Jesus said unto him, Verily I say unto thee, To-day shalt thou be with me in paradise.

—Luke 23:39-43

II
TO-DAY SHALT THOU BE WITH ME

Again we inquire, what on earth is happening here? Well, there were other crosses on that hill. There will always be other crosses on calvaries. There is never just one cross on a hill. And on these other crosses, on these extra crosses, on these more-than-the-one cross, too, "the wrong in human life" sometimes "turns in on itself," (*Curvatus in se,* said Luther) and destroys itself. The whole Christian drama demands these other crosses. The writers of all the Gospel accounts were branded by the sight of the other crosses. The extra crosses keep saying that there are times, even in this plush world of the wicked, where wickedness is rewarded. Even in this plush world of the wicked, malefactors sometimes are crucified. People do sometimes get just what they deserve. Malefactors as well as savers, are crucified. That is to say,

25

ABIGAIL E. WEEKS MEMORIAL LIBRARY
UNION COLLEGE
BARBOURVILLE, KENTUCKY

there never is, there never has been just one cross. There are all kinds of crosses.

This cross was Christ's. Yet this cross is only half of it; if it were his cross alone, humanity would be as it has always been. If the Cross were just his, his cross would make no difference. If it were his alone, says Paul Scherer, humanity would not be worth saving. But it was not just his alone. Frank Mead has Barabbas cry, thunderstruck, "Jehovah God! that's my cross he's dying on!" So it was. And this is the point, *every word they remembered that he said as he hanged there is a word of his identifying with us.* His cross is identified with us and our crosses. His cross is universal. But his cross can be univeral only because this universal cross participates. It makes him relevant by his intrinsic deed and by those with whom his cross is identified. He participates with us.

In the Easter drama, Barabbas learns that it was *God,* not the mob, who had said, "Give me Barabbas." Here we see the unfathomable mystery of human response. Here is where the war now lies. The battle is no longer for some segment of mankind. The battle is no longer just race relations. The battle is no longer just economic justice. The battle is no longer between the East and the West or between two Western perversions of economic life like communism and capitalism. The battle now lies where Walt Whitman put it. The battle is for mankind. We now have to join the whole human race. Since Christ on his cross, which was not his alone, identifies with humanity's bottom exhibit, the whole race is involved.

We could have accepted his identification with his mother or with that disciple who had such capacity for redemption. But here he identifies, as if he would include all mankind, with our bottom exhibit. What on earth is happening here?

It is so simple we almost miss it. A human being of a particularly low level is responding to his chance. This is all. A particular human being of an especially low level is responding to his high chance. Look at him. Luke says the man is *"kakourgos,"* a common criminal. Thus far in his life he has ignored his chances, just as he has ignored God. Others have denied God, and still others have tried to use God. But this man is miserably and deservedly suffering for his own sin. In the hour they come to take him to his cross he can only say, "I deserve all they do to me."

The thieves are brought along to get the executions over with on the same day. They watch Jesus crucified. They wait their own turns. Their terror mounts. Then one of them joins the railing on Jesus. "If thou be Christ, save thyself and us!" And then a strange and quite the most wonderful human thing on the hill happens. A human being of a particularly low level responds to his chance. A thief discovers God in a Crucifixion. He sees a Cross shaped like a crown.

He sees beyond this dying Christ a King. He sees a Kingdom. He recognizes a King he had ignored. He responds to the railing from that companion cross. He cries, "Dost not thou fear God?" He sees his own guilt, crying, "We receive the due reward of our deeds." He sees something new in Jesus Christ and says, "This man hath done nothing amiss." And then, in response to this vision, he repents in dawning faith and cries from his cross to the center cross, "Lord, remember me when thou comest into thy kingdom," I share a cross with you. And Jesus goes all the way to the dying thief; *"to-day,"* he says (a direct promise), "shalt thou be with me in paradise."

I have seen, in earlier days, that at the cross of Jesus Christ all men are the same. Rich man, poor man, beggarman, thief; Chinese, Japanese, German, Negro; deacon, teacher, pastor, people. I have seen all of this. And I have seen that men are not always what they seem. Nearly all my life I have been able to see that most men are not what they look like they might be: Paul, an ugly, bald, hawk-nosed, hunchbacked Jew; Socrates, the ugliest man in Athens; Alexander, a twisted dwarf in Alexandria; Peter, a crude Galilean; and John, the coarse fisherman. But here the dying thief takes our breath away. With the fantastic capacity of men of low level, he responds to his high chance.

This says to us, does it not, that God's kingdom has always been made up of men who are hopeless?

Did you ever see so hopeless a man? This thief could not live a holy life. He could not learn the Lord's Prayer or sit at the Lord's table. He could not be a member of a church, he could not be baptized. But here a particular situation says that when Jesus Christ from his cross identifies with us, he starts at the bottom, and identifies with us all. Any man, no matter how far away nor how low, is acceptable to God. Of all the hopeless men you ever saw, this one is the most hopeless. He has broken the law and now the law is breaking him. But Jesus identified himself once with a paralytic to show that the helpless might come; with a leper to show that the loathsome might come; with a prostitute to show that the debauched might come; with a Pharisee to show, I guess, that anybody could come; with a little child to show how all have to come. And now Jesus identifies himself with this thief to show how far a man may have to come.

And now the central incident of this drama at the Cross is when the thief cries, "Lord, when you come to your kingdom, keep me in your mind," and Christ answers, "This very day shalt thou be with me in paradise." It is a Persian word, this word "paradise." It was just beginning to be widely used in Palestine. Jesus uses it in the sense in which the dead are brought immediately into the presence of the Eternal. This is what he is saying, this very day we will have the same relationship in the presence of the Eternal. Now the floating miracle of human response comes back across our vision. What on earth is happening here? And the answer: God himself is what he seems and appears to be. "What he seemed to be; that he was." Here he identifies with us.

And those who stood by, just as we said before, got the leftovers. Those who stood by and could not respond divided his raiment and cast lots. Those who had joined the railing on him (They said, "He saved others; let him save himself." They said, "If thou be the Son of God, come down from the cross.") got the leftovers. Meanwhile the drama goes right on and he identifies himself with the deepest need on the hilltop and changes it forever. Those who stood by got the leftovers.

What was left?

Wine mixed with gall! It was not a gesture of derision, really. It was the same desire to soften things that followed in the Middle Ages. When a man was condemned to die by fire they used to hang a bag of gun powder around his neck, just under his beard. When the fire reached that, the explosion would snuff out his consciousness at least, and death would be more bearable. So it was that for many years, during crucifixions, they offered a cheap wine, mixed with gall, to deaden the senses. Isn't this all that was left? Everything else was between the Master and the thief, and his beloved disciples. All those who stood by could have had left over was a little something to dull the senses for the present. This they likely left, in some kind of vessel, spilling against the foot of the cross, as they turned away.

Where they crucified him, and two other with him, on either side one, and Jesus in the midst.

And Pilate wrote a title, and put it on the cross. And the writing was, JESUS OF NAZARETH THE KING OF THE JEWS. This title then read many of the Jews: for the place where Jesus was crucified was nigh to the city: and it was written in Hebrew, and Greek, and Latin. Then said the chief priests of the Jews to Pilate, Write not, The King of the Jews; but that he said, I am King of the Jews. Pilate answered, What I have written I have written.

Then the soldiers, when they had crucified Jesus, took his garments, and made four parts, to every soldier a part; and also his coat: now the coat was without seam, woven from the top throughout. They said therefore among themselves, let us not rend it, but cast lots for it, whose it shall be: that the scripture might be fulfilled, which saith, They parted my raiment among them, and for my vesture they did cast lots. These things therefore the soldiers did.

Now there stood by the cross of Jesus his mother, and his mother's sister, Mary the wife of Cleophas, and Mary Magdalene. When Jesus therefore saw his mother, and the disciple standing by, whom he loved, he saith unto his mother, Woman, behold thy son! Then saith he to the disciple, Behold thy mother! And from that hour that disciple took her unto his own home.

—John 19:18-27

provide more wine. But back of this was her eagerness for the Mission to begin. How plunged in despair she must have been at Capernaum when in contradistinction to all she had ever expected of Messiah the mission took a direction so patently the opposite of all she had hoped for. So despairing she was that apparently she joined his brothers in the conclusion that her precious Messiah had slipped a cog. They had attempted to remove him, by force if necessary, from this ministry capricious. And now this Cross!

In less than three calendar years she sees the utter collapse of the mission, and all she gets out of it, John tells it, all she gets out of it is, "He saith unto his mother, Woman, behold thy son!" And to that disciple he said, "Behold thy mother!" And from that hour that disciple takes her unto his own. (The word "home" is not in the best manuscripts.)

From that hour that disciple takes her unto his own. Small comfort, for what she had lost, to be a hanger-on in somebody's house not her own. To be the object of the charitable love and care of one to whom she is not related when she had expected to be the queen of the world! Small comfort. There is not much left over from a mission like this. But on the other hand, is there not small wonder, too little room really to wonder, at the place Christendom has given this Mary, the mother of Jesus?

It began in an early outburst in response to some

crying need from some woman-heart the Master had
ministered to in some healing way. Torn out of the
heart of some hurting woman was that first cry,
"Blessed is the womb that bare thee, and the paps
which thou hast sucked!" This was the beginning
of our love and adoration for Mary, the mother of
Christ. In the post-Resurrection church this Mary,
abandoned to the kind offices of John by the Crucifixion, became Mary, the Mother to the Faithful,
free years later to tell Luke or whoever wrote his
Gospel all the things she had kept locked up in her
heart, lest she damage God. It took a very special
woman to mother the Messiah.

As to how special she was, the early church fought,
literally fought. There are cleavages that exist to this
day as to whether Mary was *Christotokos* or *Theoto-
kos*. Was she Mother of Christ? Or was she, as the
Greek Orthodox insist, Mother of God? Whichever
it be, the church has kept her from the Cross to this
day in a very special place.

One of my teen-agers recently came into some very
special information, biological information. She told
me that it is now possible for her to believe the virgin
birth: that the right kind of chemical or electric
shock would institute the processes of cell division
from an unfertilized egg. All that is required is that
the mother have a perfect set of chromosomes so that
none of the male chromosomes would be needed to
build a perfect human body! Of course she does not

see, and I shan't disillusion her as yet, that the dogma
loses its meaning if the affair of the birth lies within
the natural course of things. But the point, the
beautiful theological point here, is that for centuries
the church has claimed just this: that Mary did have
a perfect set of chromosomes, parthenogenetically, all
the way back to Eve! And that is positively unbiologi-
cal! The only thing being said here is that we must
not arrogate to ourselves any longer the colossal
assumption that whatever else God is he is *male*.
This is Hebrew arrogance; this is male arrogance.

Carl Jung shows in many places throughout his
work a confidence that whoever and whatever God is,
there is some female there, too. So Mary has come to
stand for the female in God. And Mary, with or without her perfect set of chromosomes, whatever this
means, must also be allowed to stand for the mother in
God. Our Roman Catholic friends are seeing psycho-
logically what the mystery religions of the ancient
world knew quite well: that someone somewhere, has
to stand for the Mother in the Godhood. Millions of
people in the ancient world knew that God was
Mother before they knew that he was Father. There
is a hint of this in the Old Testament. In the book
of Isaiah does not the prophet quote God as having
said to him, "As one over whom his mother hovers
so will I hover over you?"

So Mary has come to her place in a very understandable way. Her place is secure now. Mary is a special person, everywhere, and for always. But not then. He has no garment to leave her. It was already stripped from him; he has no money, no land, no security to give her. For that matter she would be much better off with John. He has had at least two houses that we know of, and boats. But this is beside the point too. Jesus, in the hour of his death, calls to the forestage of a desperate scene his primal relation to mankind. And again, Jesus, in the hour of his death, feels no compunction whatsoever in calling on a friend for *anything*. He does not even ask John if he would be willing to accept her. He just says, "John, there she is," and he just says, "Woman, there he is." There are no contracts, no bonds, no promises, just the shared obligation of being disciple and friend. This is what it is to be disciple. There is no limit to what one can ask. In these circumstances, with no compunctions whatever, he passes over the claims of his brothers and puts her in the hands of a friend.

And the mere fact that he sees her through this blind haze, is it not like a precious kiss? The only kind of kiss he can give is to see her. It is a blessing and a sanctification which Christendom has been eager to share. But it is more, much more. How much of human life passes in little incidents!

One of the great human beings was Epictetus, once a slave, and the great source of much that is good in ancient Stoicism. Epictetus had a wish for dying: "When I die, I should like at the moment of my death to be involved in something noble, beneficial, and for the good of all mankind, and rendering what is due to every relation in my life."

How does one render what is due to his primal relation? How does one involve himself in the good of all mankind and render what is due to every relation? Christ does both. There is everything in his death that Epictetus could have wanted. He dies rendering what is due to every primal relation in life and at the same time accomplishing that that is for the good of all. He, in his dying, as in his birth, goes back into the very essence of his identification with man. He grasps from and gives to his mother. And how much closer to being man can one get?

The memory of the church includes still the recollection of A. J. Gossip, the famous preacher who used that strange text, "In the morning my wife died, and in the evening I preached to the people." With respect to his own death he said:

God grant that when the dark is falling round us in that last scene of all, when the poorest of us, for once, holds the center of the stage, we may face death with a like unselfishness—not fidgeting about ourselves, not hurriedly making last minute preparations, but packed and ready and waiting for the tide, may be able eagerly to enter into those around us . . . that for us, too, death may be no squalid thing, but big and . . . invincible.

The whole world watches this man dying. No man ever died in the presence of so many watchers. He dies for, and in view of, the whole world; and yet, in the moment of his dying, for the whole world, we see him reach out to identify with the primal of manly, human relationship. "Behold thy mother." At no point in his journey does he become more completely man than here. Nor at any point in his journey is he more completely worthy, man-wise, of being called Son of God.

My God, my God, why hast thou forsaken me? Why art thou so far from helping me, and from the words of my roaring? O my God, I cry in the daytime, but thou hearest not; and in the night season, and am not silent. . . . But I am a worm, and no man; a reproach of men, and despised of the people. All they that see me laugh me to scorn: they shoot out the lip, they shake the head, saying, He trusted on the Lord that he would deliver him: let him deliver him, seeing he delighted in him. . . . Be not far from me; for trouble is near; for there is none to help. Many bulls have compassed me: strong bulls of Bashan have beset me round. They gaped upon me with their mouths, as a ravening and a roaring lion. I am poured out like water, and all my bones are out of joint: my heart is like wax; it is melted in the midst of my bowels. My strength is dried up like a potsherd; and my tongue cleaveth to my jaws; and thou hast brought me into the dust of death. For dogs have compassed me: the assembly of the wicked have enclosed me: they pierced my hands and my feet. I may tell all my bones: they look and stare upon me. They part my garments among them, and cast lots upon my vesture. But be not thou far from me, O Lord: O my strength, haste thee to help me.

—Ps. 22:1-19

And about the ninth hour Jesus cried with a loud voice, saying, Eli, Eli, lama sabachthani? that is to say, My God, my God, why hast thou forsaken me? Some of them that stood there, when they heard that, said, This man calleth for Elias. And straightway one of them ran, and took a sponge, and filled it with vinegar, and put it on a reed, and gave him to drink.

—Matt. 27:46-48

IV

MY GOD, WHY HAST THOU FORSAKEN?

Before this stark cry, rising out of three hours of midday darkness, what is there to say? Obviously it is a cry of delirium. All conscious men have a pain threshold. Across this threshold lies the land of delirium, the realm of unreal threshing about that comes with unmitigated hurting, where no cool hands can reach. Obviously it is a cry of delirium, but more, it is a cry of desolation that is utter aloneness. Whose hand can reach here? Whose gall-soaked sponge held on a reed can dull this agony? These words he cries say that there is left in his consciousness no glimmer of the Presence of the Holy. Here all memory and hope and otherness have been wrung out of him. This is depression, utter depression. This is hysteria. Depression and hysteria always have in common this complete self-awareness. This is the

45

absolute self-centeredness of unbounded pain and
despair. Any man pierced, impaled on a stake, thinks
only of self. This is the ultimate *thereness*. This is
Heidegger's *Dasein*. This is what it is to be nailed,
halted, estopped, abandoned. This is that aloneness
where one is under the knife with no prospect of
being anywhere else. There is no elsewhere! This
is crucifixion: to be tearing apart where one is, with
no prospect of movement left, without any Other.
Obviously, it is this, but it is more.

Again, what on earth is happening here? Is it also
a cry of dereliction? Is it possible that God could
have abandoned his own? Not without denying God's
Godhood; not without doing something to his Godhood that we cannot endure. There were other cries
to God from this neighborhood. It has been only a
matter of hours since he has said, "Father, if it be
possible, let this cup pass from me." There would
be, in the next moment, another cry to God, *"Pater
in manu tuas,"* we hear it sung at Eastertide. "Father,
into thy hands I commend my spirit." God heard
the first cry (Father, if it be possible, let this cup
pass). God heard the other cry (Father, into thy
hands, I commend my spirit), and he will hear the
startling cry, "It is finished," from lungs that were
already dead. Where is *he* now? In this "My God,
my God," where is he?

What if this cry, "My God, my God," is not addressed to God at all? What if he is not talking to

God, but to us? What if the "My God, my God, why hast thou forsaken me" is addressed to us who "sitting down watched him *there*"? What if this cry is an appeal to us, not a cry to God at all? What if it is not a *delirium?* What if it is not a *desolation?* What if it is most certainly not *dereliction?* What if it is *identification!*

Every Jew on that hillside knew the classic song of Messiah. It was as familiar to them as "Mary Had a Little Lamb" is to us. Jesus our Lord is not so much crying as he is quoting. He is not so much calling on God, as he is identifying with us in the classic Psalm of the Messiah that every Jew had memorized. "Look," he says, "look at what is happening here!" This is what it is to be utterly man, left to your own resources. This is what it is to be derelict, desolate, empty. This is what it is to be Jew; this is what it is to be utterly Redeemer; this is what it is to be utterly *where we are!* Here Jesus Christ is identifying himself. Not with man, but as Man. He is man as he is always when left utterly to his own resources.

What on earth is happening here? Here the Incarnation reaches bottom, there is no way to go from here but up. There is no lower floor; this is the ground floor of manhood. Here, in utter dereliction and desolation, he is *us!* Here he identifies with the Messiah of Ps. 22; here he joins Jewishness, here he calls on all history to recognize him; here he joins what it is to be man; here he identifies with ultimate manhood left to its own resources. And God is there, never more there, or here, even in Creation, than there!

Patripassianism is one of the classic heresies dedicated to the idea that God is always only One. The Patripassians merged Christ with the Father. This view of Bishop Calixtus, later Pope Calixtus, with Noetus and Praxeas, the Chalcedonian formula outlawed. They threw out at Chalcedon the view that Christ and the Father are one and the same. But a vestige remains of this heresy to grace our modern view of atonement, which permits us at least to say that *God was never more anywhere than here!*

Buttrick reports somewhere in a sermon of his that there hangs in a chapel in Milan an early Renaissance painting of the Crucifixion in which, late in the evening, when the light allows it, from a certain angle, a shadowy figure seems to have been interposed between Christ and the wood of the cross. The artist was trying to say, the *Father was there too!* So, when Jesus says, "My God, My God, why hast thou forsaken me?" he is also saying, is he not, look what is happening here? But he is saying more to those who knew the song by memory:

He is saying: "They cried unto thee and were delivered!" He is saying, "Be not thou far from me, O Lord!" He is saying, "All the ends of the world shall remember and turn unto the Lord." Although the cry is a cry of ultimate identification, he cannot be more man than this; he cannot join Jewish hope and expectation more fully than this. He is Jewishness personified!

Mark, in his Gospel, gives the cry in Aramaic. In the classic Hebrew the word Eli, Eli now reads, *Eloi, Eloi!* Could *any* Jew have heard this Aramaic *Eloi* and have confused it for *"Elijah"?* They heard him cry *Eli, Eli!* or *Eloi, Eloi!* and said "This fellow is calling for Elijah." In the Semitic world to this day, Elijah is the Eternal Wanderer who always comes to the Semite when he is at the end of his road. They heard him say, *"Elijah, Elijah!"* Could any true Jew have heard him say *Eloi* and have thought it to have been *Elijah?* I do not know. I just know that men can hear anything they wish to hear. In church, especially, men can always hear most anything. Those who heard his cry, knew him. Those who had no wish to hear, those who had no hope of hearing, heard him call Elijah, and ran to substitute vinegar.

It is still the same with us. Most of us have to live on the leftovers around the Cross: the wine and the gall, the vinegar left over, and the poor clothes they divided. These are all worn, they are just leftovers, for those who cannot hear. But for those who heard, in the context of identification, they shall never have to say, "My God, my God, why hast thou forsaken me," in the context of ultimate dereliction. They will always be saying it in the context of the rest of

this Psalm he quoted, "They cried unto thee and
were delivered!" Although here in this Psalm, and
in this Cross, we do hear man at the uttermost end
of the earth, cut off from his Eternal. O yes! But we
hear him also saying, "Look, no man from this point
ever has to cry except in the context that "all the
ends of the world shall remember and turn unto the
Lord." For God was there.

Save me, O God; for the waters are come in unto my soul. I sink in deep mire, where there is no standing: I am come into deep waters, where the floods overflow me. I am weary of my crying: my throat is dried: mine eyes fail while I wait for my God. They that hate me without a cause are more than the hairs of mine head: they that would destroy me, being mine enemies wrongfully, are mighty: then I restored that which I took not away. O God, thou knowest my foolishness; and my sins are not hid from thee. Let not them that wait on thee, O Lord God of hosts, be ashamed for my sake: let not those that seek thee be confounded for my sake, O God of Israel. Because for thy sake I have borne reproach; shame hath covered my face. I am become a stranger unto my brethren, and an alien unto my mother's children. For the zeal of thine house hath eaten me up; and the reproaches of them that reproached thee are fallen upon me. When I wept, and chastened my soul with fasting, that was to my reproach. I made sackcloth also my garment; and I became a proverb to them. They that sit in the gate speak against me; and I was the song of the drunkards. But as for me, my prayer is unto thee, O Lord, in an acceptable time: O God, in the multitude of thy mercy hear me, in the truth of thy salvation. Deliver me out of the mire, and let me not sink: let me be delivered from them that hate me, and out of the deep waters. Let not the waterflood overflow me, neither let the deep swallow me up, and let not the pit shut her mouth upon me. Hear me, O Lord; for thy lovingkindness is good: turn unto me according to the multitude of thy tender mercies. And hide not thy face from thy servant; for I am in trouble: hear me speedily. Draw nigh unto my soul, and redeem it: deliver me because of mine enemies. Thou hast known my reproach, and my shame, and my dishonour: mine adversaries are all before thee. Reproach hath broken my heart; and I am full of heaviness: and I looked for some to take pity, but there was none; and for comforters, but I found none. They gave me also gall for my meat; and in my thirst they gave me vinegar to drink.

—Ps. 69:1-21

After this, Jesus knowing that all things were now accomplished, that the scripture might be fulfilled, saith, I thirst. . . . and they filled a sponge with vinegar, and put it upon [a stalk], and put it to his mouth. When Jesus therefore had received the vinegar, he said, It is finished.

—John 19:28-30

V

I THIRST

Somehow it has never seemed right for Messiah to have been so thirsty. We recall that his ministry really opened at a well in Samaria with Messiah asking for drink. "Give me to drink," he said to a Samaritan woman of the street, then talked the morning out about a coming kingdom. He began his ministry asking for water, and now as his agony closes the next to last word used is of Messiah asking for water. In between he has played on thirst as a theme all the while. Like a great common denominator is thirst.

Of course it is a dry and thirsty land, with few wells. Of course to drink is a perennial problem. For thousands of years the classic greeting has been to ask for water and the classic gesture of hospitality has been to give water. But he must have had a prodigious thirst.

This cry, "I thirst," what it must have done to
Mary! Perhaps for her this was the worst cry to bear.
To hear a little boy cry in the dark night, "I am
thirsty," and to be unable to give him water, this
would be the worst of all. Michelangelo's moving
"Pieta" which the Pope is allowing to come to New
York shows a shrunken Christ. After death it is a
smaller Christ which is drawn across his mother's lap.
This must have been the worst word of all, to hear a
little boy cry in the dark night, "I am thirsty."

Once several years ago, in Jackson, Mississippi,
my old teacher heard someone's little boy crying on
the floor below, in a public house, a hotel. He got
up and went to see about him; for who can stand it
when a little boy cries for water?

How overwhelming this thirst, to cut through all
his other agonies. Strange how thirsty he could be
even when this was the least of the pain. But do we
not have on our hands here a Messiah obsessed with
thirst? "Blessed are they which do hunger and *thirst*
after righteousness: for they shall be filled," he has
said. "Whosoever drinketh of this water shall *thirst*
again: but whosoever drinketh of the water that I
shall give him shall never *thirst;* but the water that
I shall give him shall be in him a well of water spring-
ing up into everlasting life." "He that believeth on
me shall never *thirst,*" he has said. "If any man *thirst,*
let him come unto me, and drink." He began by
saying, "Give me to drink." He closes saying that he

is still thirsty. And in between there lies the aching
thirst for a coming kingdom that he said was served
by any cup of cold water given anyone in his name.
How thirsty can Messiah be and still be Messiah? How
needy and weak and human?

Two questions: First, does this thirst he confesses
on Calvary have anything to do with the thirst he has
power to quench? And the answer obviously is no,
they are not connected. We overspiritualize in some
dreadful sense to play so on this thirst. Yet again, what
on earth is happening here? In some grand sense, we
cannot deny that he here hallows every little boy's
nighttime thirst. He here makes a sacrament out of
every glass of water. He here makes a priest out of
every stumbling sleepy father, and out of every groan-
ing mother, who slopping glass in hand moves
through the dark hall from water tap to a little fellow's
bed. He makes you a priest or a priestess. I'm saying,
you, who have your nighttime thirst, ought not to be
able to drink without remembering this sacrament of
the thirst. You ought not to be able to bend over a
water fountain without remembering what it is to
thirst.

Second, does this thirst have anything to do with
that God-intoxication, that God-drunkness, that in-
satiable God-thirst of Israel's history? No. Once more
we are overspiritualizing to hang this on the little
phrase, "I thirst." And yet Ps. 69, which he seems to
have known, tells of another man strung up, for it

says, "They gave me also gall for my meat; and in my thirst they gave me vinegar to drink." Is there not in the sixty-ninth psalm the whole construct of a coming kingdom lying strongly in view?

Is it possible that when he says, "I thirst," even as when he said, "My God, why hast thou forsaken me," that he quoted. There is a *double* identifying here. I see him identifying with the thirst of all Israel, and with her messianic hopes as well. I see him identifying himself with the coming kingdom, and this event on Calvary with the situation of the sufferer in the sixty-ninth psalm. For his simple phrase "I thirst" becomes a sign pointed to that haunting cry in a dry and thirsty land where no water is. That haunting cry, I thirst, becomes I "whom they have pierced." When he says, "I thirst," he's saying he is the soul of the sixty-ninth psalm. It is an identification with all the hope Israel ever has had which posited a Messiah in a dry and thirsty land where no water is—just vinegar.

There is a double identification here. For not only does he identify with all the hope of Israel, he identifies with every human need. Biologically this is your most fundamental need, water. And here he is with us. I don't know what you know about life and about dying. But isn't this about the last thing a man can be—thirsty? And isn't this about the last of one's powers—to drink? Here, on the cross, the Messiah has run out the end of this human track. Here in the cry, "I thirst," is the end of the track for all human

beings. He has come all the way. There isn't anywhere to go. He has come to the end of human ability
and resources and stands wholly identified with us.
When he gives his utterly human cry, "Father, into
thy hands," and the poignant, "It is finished," he is
past the end.

Now of all those who stood by hearing and not
hearing, taking the leftovers of his poor clothing or
that first spilled-out vinegar that he rejected—of all
those who stood by with the leftovers, which would
you rather have been? The lad who ran and got the
vinegar for him to drink? I think so. Here is maybe
the only leftover worth keeping. Do you suppose that
Jesus knew when he said, "he who gives you a cup of
water in my name serves the kingdom"? Do you suppose he had any way of knowing that someday a lad
or a Roman soldier or a young Jew would run and get
something for him to wet his thirst? Of all those who
stood by, I suppose, I would rather have been the one
who ran and got him something to drink.

And it was about the sixth hour, and there was a darkness over all the earth until the ninth hour. And the sun was darkened, and the veil of the temple was rent in the midst.

And when Jesus had cried with a loud voice, he said, Father, into thy hands I commend my spirit: and having said thus, he gave up the ghost.

—Luke 23:44-46

VI

FATHER, INTO THY HANDS

What on earth is happening here? We have come here, have we not, to the end of track? This is where manhood runs out; this is where there is no other place to go. This is the human-boundary situation. The Son of God, I think, did not die by some fiat of God's will to buy off Satan. The Son of God did not die to satisfy a pagan god of legal righteousness. He did not die to ransom a kidnaped man. Nor did he die to keep me from having to die. Rather he died because I have to die. This is what it is to be man: to have to die. He became a man and followed manhood to the end of its track. And just where we, too, can no longer see anything, by an act of faith he turned the outcome of his venture over to the Father. The end of track occurred for him just where it comes for us. Where Death, and Evil, as ultimates, have to be faced without even a club left in our hands. Here there is nothing with which to fight anymore. No ambition, no ego, no pride, no will, no strength, no desire, no breath. This is where the end of track always comes. Where, I say, we are left without a club in hand with which to beat off evil; here sans strength, sans ego, sans will, desire, and breath, we, too, have nothing left to say but, "Father, into thy hands I give over my spirit." He hangs here, at edge of dark, where all our humanisms ultimately run out.

Karl Barth, in a magnificent introduction to a reprint of Ludwig Feuerbach's *The Essence of Christianity,* perhaps the most dangerous book of the last four centuries, calls back to light Ehrenberg's devastating criticism of Feuerbach. Ehrenberg had said that with respect to death Feuerbach was a *Nichtkenner.* And with respect to evil, he was a *Verkenner.* He did not know death, and he mis-knew evil. Therefore he could not help us. He was both *notknower* and *mis-knower.* At this place then, where we do not-know death, and where we mis-know evil, where all our subterfuges and defenses run out on us, at this human end of track, we say, "Father, into thy hands."

But listen, it is not as if the Son of God went his whole life and then called on God when time was gone. It is not as if God the Father had never heard his voice before. This is no deathbed baptism. Did

not he always call on God? Nor is it, I think, as if
he calls on One who had been absent from him a
moment before. Just an ordinary statement is implied.
"Father, into thy hands I commend my spirit." It is
as if he were saying, "Here at this exhaustion of
strength and time, here where all strength, will, ego,
ambition, pride, thrust, and power have run out,
here at this exhausting of strength and time, whatever there is of meaning and of future is in the hands
of my Father." What is there more to be said, than
this?

The wilderness and the solitary place shall be glad for them; and the desert shall rejoice, and blossom as the rose. It shall blossom abundantly, and rejoice even with joy and singing: the glory of Lebanon shall be given unto it, the excellency of Carmel and Sharon, they shall see the glory of the Lord, and the excellency of our God.

Strengthen ye the weak hands, and confirm the feeble knees. Say to them that are of a fearful heart, Be strong, fear not: behold, your God will come with vengeance, even God with a recompence; he will come and save you. Then the eyes of the blind shall be opened, and the ears of the deaf shall be unstopped. Then shall the lame man leap as an hart, and the tongue of the dumb sing: for in the wilderness shall waters break out, and streams in the desert. And the parched ground shall become a pool, and the thirsty land springs of water: in the habitation of dragons, where each lay, shall be grass with reeds and rushes. And an highway shall be there, and a way, and it shall be called The way of holiness; the unclean shall not pass over it; but it shall be for those: the wayfaring men, though fools, shall not err therein. No lion shall be there, nor any ravenous beast shall go up thereon, it shall not be found there; but the redeemed shall walk there: And the ransomed of the Lord shall return, and come to Zion with songs and everlasting joy upon their heads: they shall obtain joy and gladness, and sorrow and sighing shall flee away.

—Isa. 35:1-10

When Jesus therefore had received the vinegar, he said, It is finished: and he bowed his head, and gave up the ghost. —John 19:30

VII

IT IS FINISHED

There are two cries in the life of our Lord, two wildly exultant cries. Again, as with that thirst, though there is no real connection, I am sure, they come at the opening of his ministry and at the close. *"Upage, Satana,"* he had cried, "Go down, Satan!" "Get thee behind me, Satan!" And now this wild cry, *"Tetelestai!"* "It is finished!" Both the "Go down, Satan" and the "It is finished" were uttered following days of despair and desolation. The one exulting cry followed forty days of hunger and temptation and decision. The other followed twenty-four hours of taunting misery and trial and crucifixion. Both of these are cries of identification. This man is identifying himself with something and somebody. In both instances, he is exultingly accepting something in the presence of God. "Go down, Satan," as man with man I can withstand all your assaults, he is saying, on the closing of that third temptation when the evil ruler offered him the world. And this "It is finished!" is the exulting discovery that as man with man he could lay out a life as God intended a life to be laid out. He could finish.

Who can finish anything? We finish nothing. John Ruskin claimed that his best finishing was but a coarse and blundering work. And what is finished here? The perfect life, we say, and this is right. The highway Isaiah had foretold and John the Baptist had cleared. There shall be a highway and a way, they had said. This shall be called "The way of holiness." No lion shall walk there, nor any ravenous beast. The ransomed shall walk there singing; they shall return, and joy and gladness shall be upon their heads.

In the early centuries those who were mere bishops of the church at Rome cast about for a high title that would express a new, exalted position. They came onto the phrase, *pontifex maximus*. We still hear it today in terms of the Supreme Pontiff. But it simply meant *"bridge builder,"* the great bridge builder. It was a title taken not only from the Roman Empire, the word for Caesars, but it was a word intended to describe the mighty bridging that had gone on when Jesus Christ cried, "It is finished."

These are all high and worthy answers to our query as to what is finished. We could answer it in terms of the perfect life. We could answer it in terms of the highway, the highway to the Kingdom. We could answer it in terms of the great bridge. But there is another answer, and a larger one.

Just as he has used thirst so frequently as a figure of desire, so now he uses cup as a figure of salvation. What is finished? His identification within a crucible of redemption is finished. Here when he cries, "It is finished," for the first time in man's long history, man is Man. This is the first Man. All who have gone before him have just been Adam. Adam is the head of nothing. Adam is the father of nothing for us but trouble. Who follows Adam? Who believes in Adam? The Old Adam and the Old Nick in us are synony-mous terms since Niccolò Machiavelli gave us a human devil. But Old Adam is the same; he deserves to be head of nothing. He is not head of the race. "It is finished!" Jesus Christ is the first man. Jesus Christ is the true man. Jesus is the head of the race. What is finished? *The race has been perfected.*

This identification of his, however, comes to its fulfillment in what we can best call a crucible or a chalice or a cup. The cup of salvation is finished. The cup of redemption is finished. The crucible is com-pleted. Six weeks before when James and John's mother, Salome, had asked him if her sons might be the first ones in his kingdom, one on his right and one on his left, he had asked them, Are you able to drink of the cup which I am on the verge of drinking? A few hours before this, had he not prayed, "O

Father, if it be possible, let this cup pass from me"?
Now here, he lifts the empty cup to the Father's view.
And not a drop of the gall is left. He had finished.
O Father, if it be possible, let me pass this cup. Here he
holds up the cup to show the Father that the full cup
of manhood is swallowed. He has trod the wine press
of the wrath of Almighty God, alone. Not a drop is
left. The cup is empty. Finished, all gone. See, not
à drop is left; the hemlock is gone. There is no more
identifying he can do. He is now *with us*. He is now
for us. He is now *in us*. And this is why he is dead.
For this is what it is to be identified with us. It is to
be dying, dead. And here only the Father can do
anything at all.

All the others tried, did they not? Joseph of Ari-
mathaea, who loved him, "but secretly for fear of the
Jews," and the aristocrat, Nicodemus, went boldly
to Pilate and said, "We want the body of that Rabbi."
Pilate said, "Take it away, we are done with it." But
the women said scent it and wrap it and care tenderly
for it and weep over it, for all we have got is a dead
body. He had identified. The rest, if there is any
rest, if there is another act, the rest of it is God's.

The kingdoms of this world are become the kingdoms of our Lord, and of his Christ; and he shall reign for ever and ever.

—Rev. 11:15

After these things Jesus shewed himself again to the disciples at the sea of Tiberias; and on this wise shewed he himself.

—John 21:1

Be thou partaker of the afflictions of the gospel according to the power of God; Who hath saved us, and called us with an holy calling, not according to our works, but according to his own purpose and grace, which was given us in Christ Jesus before the world began, but is now made manifest by the appearing of our Saviour

Jesus Christ, who hath abolished death, and hath brought life and immortality to light through the gospel.
—II Tim. 1:8*b*-10

Behold, I shew you a mystery; we shall not all sleep, but we shall all be changed.
—I Cor. 15:51

We give thee thanks, O Lord God Almighty, which art, and wast, and art to come; because thou hast taken to thee thy great power, and hast reigned.
—Rev. 11:17

VIII

BEHOLD, I SHOW YOU A MYSTERY

From where he had stood on Olivet, and from where his corpse hangs on Golgotha, with that long week of identification in between, how futile this talk of a kingdom to come. How unthinkable that his suffering and death should be participant, even determinative, factors in that coming kingdom. What on earth has happened here, and what can happen now?

Faith has to look too far, and across such torn terrain. So many things seem to have been decided on such inconsequentials: a sunken road at Waterloo, snowflakes before Moscow, orders wrapped around a lost cigar at Antietam—yet ends are always present in beginnings. There are always predetermining factors, and it is so with his coming kingdom now viewed from Calvary.

This is faith's long look. It doesn't believe in time; it believes in God. It doesn't believe in wars that are lost by battles; it believes in a war won before its battles are fought. Faith can wait. Faith can lose everything—everything but hope. But from here, hope is lost, and this is the stupendous wonder of those words: *"After these things"*!

After these things," it begins casually. After what things? After they had stood at a little distance and watched that lone white body hanging between heaven and earth and had turned their heads and bowed their backs and retched up the last bitter dregs of their kingdom. After they had turned back to their Galilean rabbit hutches. After that half-born Nicodemus, with Joseph, had said to Pilate, "Give us that rabbi corpse." After split veils and dark heavens and the lonesome cry, "It is finished," had been muffled in a sealed tomb. After those believable, perfectly believable things, certainly.

What is totally incredible is that within the same century a desperately serious writing should be claiming, "The kingdoms of this world are become the kingdoms of our Lord, and of his Christ; and he shall reign for ever and ever." And just here we lose our nerve. Unless there are really some other "after . . . things," we cannot see him reigning anywhere "for ever and ever." Unless the word did filter down a roadway that the women had found an emptied tomb; unless two on an Emmaus journey did hear him say "O fools, and slow of heart and head, ought not the Christ to have been identified in the suffering . . ." Unless he did, after such things, show himself "alive again to his disciples."

How did this immortality bit, with Rest Lawn Cemeteries and Nirvana Mausoleums ever get mixed up in *this?* The New Testament is talking of something else—a Kingdom and a *Resurrection!* This means infinitely more than immortality. But the New Testament knows nothing of a Resurrection that is separated by more than a hyphen from a Cross.

From the very beginning there is no resurrection without a cross. We are "partakers in the afflictions native to the gospel." We are to be identified with the tensions that make a Cross inevitable and are the inseparable, undetached preamble to Resurrection. No Cross, no crown! From the beginning of the gospel this is so. There is an identification to be made here.

Immortality is not resurrection. Resurrection implies something else. This is resurrection brought into the service of *life* and *light,* as Greek liturgy knows, and this is something else. It means there is no such thing as a cross-less resurrection. It means that the very tensions of creation are involved; that everything that can die does die. It means that a cross gets everything that lives. It means that nothing survives by any other route than ordeal, tension, cross. It means that *crisis* (cross) is written in for

insitutions, governments, ideas, persons; even truth
lives on crosses of contradiction. Everything that
survives goes the way of this New Testament pattern:
ordeal, catharsis, charisma, to Resurrection. The way
is the cross-way: cross, cleansing, grace, new life!

Jesus Christ came to give this process meaning.
Those who have been identified with his life find in
him the cosmic demonstration of the eternal meaning
of cross, suffering, cleansing, grace, new life. He came
to show in himself the process that leads to any eternal
for all races, all cultures, all men. In him all life
meanings subsist and are demonstrated. From him
the pattern can be made intelligible.

All history now reveals this cross, suffering, cleansing, grace, new life pattern. All human experience
justifies it. Even the stars in the heaven are in or have
been through their process of fiery burning cross.
The power of reason exists only to cut everything
away that can be cut from all our substitutes for
truth.

Jesus Christ is the hero with a thousand faces
sought by all people as the clue to man's life
and travail. When the world is finished it will be
Christ's world though it may well not be a "Christian" world. As never before, he is Redeemer,
Saviour, Exemplar, Leader, Master, Son of God sent
to lead us through our crosses that we might look
like sons of God too. Sent to make all religion

except truth untenable, the faith teaches that in *him* any man who will give himself to this understanding of his own crosses, his own ordeals, his own sufferings, can find in his own sufferings such a charismatic cleansing that he is never the same as he would have been without this cross. He walks his day's journey participating in new life that erupts after every crisis.

Any man who finds this, finds his own creative function being fulfilled—wherever he is—finds his own enduring destiny being consummated, and his own personal powers begin to taste like eternal powers. Here Christ becomes God's meaning, life's meaning, and in our believing surrender he becomes our personal contemporary, companion, possession. And only by the appropriation of this meaning of cross and suffering, cleansing and grace, in order to taste new life, can any human being transcend the inexorable or surmount the inevitable. Only here is it true that "Though my body be destroyed, yet shall I see."

And here I run into trouble, for I have a sin of fear.

I have a sinne of feare, that when I have spunne
My last thred, I shall perish on the shore.

To this my fear the gospel speaks under three audacious banners with which I am called to identify:

Incarnation-invasion—that God who loves, loves so that he has invaded us, has come to identify with us.

Crucifixion-redemption—that in the identification of God with our splitness there could come the healing to wholeness of the whole race, even me.

Death-resurrection—that there is no end to anything until God finishes it. Salvation is created! Redemption is completion of creation. For *behold, I show you a mystery,* he says.

All we had to begin on was that pathetic journey against the towers of Jerusalem and his cry, "O Jerusalem, Jerusalem, . . . how often would I have gathered thy children together as a hen doth gather her brood."

The New English Bible transposes that spectacular claim, made surely within the same century, "The sovereignty of the world has passed to our Lord and his Christ, and he shall reign for ever and ever!"

Has it now? For there follows, even in the Book, a woman robed with the sun, pregnant and in anguish; a red dragon with seven heads and ten horns knocking down a third of the stars with its tail; the war of Michael and the dragon Angels; a beast like a leopard with feet like a bear, the mouth of a lion, and a scar in his head; there follows a lamb on Mount Zion, and the cry, Stretch out your sickle and reap for earth's harvest is overripe—but we do not yet

see the world subject unto him, mourns the book of
Hebrews.

Yet: you cannot conduct your business without
being aware where you have gone counter to him.

You cannot live with your wife or without your
wife except as you are conscious of his claims upon
her and you and for you.

You cannot vote your conscience without wishing
for a better choice to offer to him, or secretly wishing
you could vote *for* him.

You cannot conceive of an earthly unity that is not
to be marked by his spirit.

And, if you do not believe him at all, you wish
you could. If you do not obey him, you know you
would be better if you did. Even if you think he
never was, you wish he had been, or hope he will be.
And you know that if man is ever truly man, he
will be like him. He has won. The kingdoms of this
earth have become—

Yet they have not. But if they have not, after two
thousand years, why have they not disposed of him?
Why is he here to haunt us with the not yet? Why
has there been achieved no oneness of even the evil
kingdoms? Why is he still in the world? How so many
devilish and divided centers of power? If no evil
kingdom has been achieved and the war of Michael
and the dragon Angels is not done until he is ulti-

mately master, could the secret be in his identification of himself with us and with ours and that he still abides in us where the warfare is at his highest?

We give thee thanks, O Lord God Almighty, which are, and wast, and art to come; because thou hast taken to thee thy great power, and hast reigned! AMEN.

ABIGAIL E. WEEKS MEMORIAL LIBRARY
UNION COLLEGE
BARBOURVILLE, KENTUCKY